Original title:
Treetop Tales

Copyright © 2025 Creative Arts Management OÜ
All rights reserved.

Author: Colin Harrington
ISBN HARDBACK: 978-1-80567-233-3
ISBN PAPERBACK: 978-1-80567-532-7

The Language of Twigs and Leaves

In the chat of branches tall,
A twig whispers, 'Hear my call!'
The leaves giggle in delight,
As squirrels dance from left to right.

Branches creak a tune so weird,
'Keep it down, you know we're feared!'
But owls chuckle, wisdom spread,
'Just join the party, use your head!'

Poems Beyond the Forest Floor

A caterpillar makes a rhyme,
Says, 'I'll be a butterfly, in time!'
Then slips on leaves, all slick and slim,
The forest floor laughs, 'Go on, swim!'

With every wiggle, dreams take flight,
As mushrooms join the funky night.
Raccoons read lines, not one's a bore,
They dance like they just won the score!

Glimmers of Light Among the Branches

Fireflies spark like little stars,
They argue 'bout their flashy cars.
One zips by, with a wink so bright,
'Hey guys, I'm the fastest tonight!'

The moon laughs down from its high seat,
As crickets tap their tiny feet.
Says one to two, 'Now don't be shy,
Let's join this race, give it a try!'

Selves of the Swaying Grove

The trees sway in a silly dance,
'Look at me, I've got the chance!'
Their roots trip up, a foot or two,
As branches twirl, they sing, 'Whee-hoo!'

Saplings giggle with glee galore,
'You think you're cool? Just check the score!'
With every sway, the laughter grows,
In this tall tale, anything goes!

Echoing through the Arboreal Realm

Squirrels chatter, what a scene,
Jumping branches, bold and keen.
With acorns tossed as flying snacks,
They stage a war, there's no relax.

Birds on branches sing their tunes,
Dodging giggles of some raccoons.
With each note, a leafy dance,
Nature laughs, it takes a chance.

Wings and Whispers

The butterflies wear silly hats,
They flutter by with giggling chats.
Bees in shades of polka dots,
Buzzing jokes, connecting thoughts.

A parrot tells a knock-knock joke,
Even trees start to poke and poke.
With every laugh, the winds do sway,
As leaves join in on the fun ballet.

Secrets of the Floating Fronds

Treetops hide their chuckling lore,
Where monkeys swing to score some more.
They toss the fruits with merry cheer,
And giggle when they land too near.

Rabbits peek, they want a taste,
But bounce away in a hasty haste.
Nature's sweetness in each prank,
With laughter, they all fill the tank.

A Symphony of Colors in the Canopy

Colors clash in leafy games,
Pinks and purples, silly names.
A chameleon thinks he's a star,
Wears plaid and stripes, it's gone too far!

The sunlight giggles with delight,
Painted leaves, a dazzling sight.
In this world of greens and bright,
Each moment sings, a pure delight.

A Dance Among the Twigs

The squirrels put on quite a show,
With tiny feet that tiptoe slow.
A waltz beneath the branches wide,
As acorns tumble, they all glide.

Chirping birds join in the fun,
Flapping wings just like a gun.
They boogie, prompt another spin,
While curious cats peek from the inn.

Rabbits hop in joy and glee,
Swinging low, as free as can be.
In this lively, leafy spree,
Nature's jesters roam with glee.

A wise old owl gives a hoot,
Rolling eyes at the silly route.
He laughs to see their wild displays,
And nods along to silly ways.

Legends of the Verdant Spire

Once atop the tallest tree,
Lived a raccoon, full of glee.
He spun tales of treasure rare,
While birds chuckled, light as air.

A curious crow, bold and spry,
Swooped in low and asked him why.
"Where's the gold that you proclaim?"
The raccoon smiled and played the game.

The legend grew, it spread like fire,
Of hidden loot and wild desire.
But all they found was nuts and seeds,
While giggles echoed through the reeds.

Each twisty trunk held secrets deep,
With critters joining in a heap.
Together they would laugh and cheer,
As mythical tales brought good cheer.

Voices in the Timber

In the grove where chatter reigns,
You hear the songs of silly trains.
Chipmunks recite their best tales,
As their laughter through the forest sails.

"Once I saw a dancing fox,"
Squeaked the squirrel, "He lost his socks!"
The bear rolled over, barely awake,
As giggles froze, the silence broke.

The laughter echoed through the pines,
In nature's hall, where joy aligns.
Each vibrant voice, a rich delight,
As critters bask in pure delight.

Old trees shake their leafy heads,
At shenanigans beneath their spreads.
With every whisper in the breeze,
The woodland hums with memories.

Tales of the Skyward Leaves

The leaves are scribbling on the breeze,
In whispers soft, like rustling seas.
Each flutter tells a jolly jest,
While critters pause to hear the rest.

A mischief-maker, the bluebird sings,
Of acorns that wore sparkly rings.
While the raccoons snicker in the shade,
At all the silly games they played.

"It's a party every sunny day!"
The babbling brook seems to say.
With tiny feet and wings that twirl,
The forest dances, a merry girl.

Skyward dreams in branches sway,
With laughter echoing all the way.
In leafy realms, let joy arise,
Underneath the endless skies.

Threads of Nature's Heart

In the woods, a squirrel prances,
Gathering nuts as he dances.
He slips, he trips, he tumbles down,
Bouncing up like a furry clown.

A raccoon peers with a cheeky grin,
Stealing snacks from the trash bin.
With acorns flying all around,
The laughter echoes, nature's sound.

Symphonies of Wood and Wind

A bird sings off-key, what a surprise,
While a ladybug winks with tiny eyes.
The branches sway, they groove and shake,
As the wind joins in, for fun's own sake.

A frog in the pond gives a loud croak,
Joking with fish, it's a real hoax.
Together they form a playful band,
Nature's music, so wild and grand.

Time in the Upper Perches

High above, where the air is light,
A wise old owl blinks with delight.
He counts the stars with a feathered hand,
Confused at times, can't understand.

A thrill-seeking parrot flies by fast,
Yelling jokes, they're a hoot and blast.
Branches shake, and giggles spread,
As the forest chortles, never dread.

The Constellation of Leaves

Leaves swirl down in a playful spin,
A dance of colors, where joy begins.
A chipmunk shimmies, then hops in place,
Creating laughter in this leafy space.

A butterfly flutters, jokingly shy,
Tickling noses as it zooms by.
Together they twirl, this troupe so bold,
With tales of wonder, forever told.

Glimpses of the Verdant Vault

In the branches, squirrels chatter,
With acorns big, they think they're fatter.
A bird tries to steal a scene,
But lands, alas, in a mess of green.

The leaves shake with laughter so loud,
While a frog leaps up, feeling proud.
A wise old owl has seen it all,
And chuckles softly at their sprawl.

A raccoon dons a leafy crown,
Strutting through like he owns the town.
He trips on roots, gives a squeak,
Then rolls away, a playful freak.

Among the vines, the laughter flows,
As nature dances with silly toes.
Every glance from the leafy heights,
Reveals a world of comedic sights.

The Riddle of the Rustling Foliage

Who tickles leaves and makes them giggle?
A sneaky breeze, or is it a wiggle?
The branches twist in a silly jest,
As acorns play hide and seek with the rest.

A chipmunk wears a nutty grin,
With pockets loaded, he wants to win.
The trees whisper secrets, oh so sly,
While a family of birds watches nearby.

A leaf falls down, a gentle tease,
Landing right on a bumblebee's knees.
The forest chuckles, they all agree,
That mischief thrives in their canopy.

Buddies gather, laughing away,
In the woodland's embrace, they choose to play.
Nature's riddle is quite a game,
Full of humor, never the same.

Skylark Serenades

Up high where the sky meets the climb,
A skylark sings of nonsense and rhyme.
With every note, a feathered prank,
He dives through clouds like a playful tank.

His buddy, the finch, tries to keep pace,
But trips on branches, oh what a face!
They whirl and twirl in a funny flight,
Chasing shadows, morning to night.

A squirrel joins in, with acrobatic flair,
Flipping and flopping, without a care.
In this trio of laughter so bright,
Every misstep brings more delight.

The wind hums a tune, oh so sweet,
As creatures gather for a grand treat.
High in the branches, joy fills the air,
In this merry madness, nothing compares.

Memoirs from the Timberline

At the peak, where tall trees sway,
A wise old crow has much to say.
His stories tickle the ears of friends,
Of wacky wanderers and their fateful ends.

A bear in glasses reads every sign,
Mistakes a tree stump for a wine dine.
The crowd erupts in raucous glee,
What fun it is to be wild and free!

The pine cones drop like comic bombs,
While chipmunks gather, sharing charms.
Each nutty tale worth a guffaw,
Leaves even the toughest in awe.

So when you wander beneath the sky,
Listen closely, don't let time fly.
Nature's memoirs, both silly and grand,
Unfold in laughter across the land.

Weavings of the Woodland

In the branches high, a squirrel pranced,
With acorn hats, they all danced.
A raccoon did a moonlit glide,
While a chipmunk giggled, tucked inside.

The wise old owl with a funky stare,
Said, "Who has time for a bit of flair?"
A deer in shades made quite the scene,
Sipping nectar from a flower, so green.

Beneath a mushroom, a hedgehog rolled,
Telling stories of treasures untold.
The laughter echoed, oh what a sight,
As fireflies joined in, glowing bright.

With whispers soft, the woods did cheer,
Celebrating mischief, far and near.
The canopy chuckled, sharing the fun,
In the heart of the woods, joy was spun.

Soft Whispers in Oak and Pine

Beneath oak leaves, a turkey danced,
While the pine tree swayed and pranced.
A rabbit in boots tried to keep time,
Clumsily hopping to a rhyme.

A crow in glasses, looking quite smart,
Balanced a book, playing the part.
He squawked out riddles, all in good jest,
While otters giggled, they were impressed.

The trees all leaned in to hear the joke,
As a frog croaked loud, it made them choke.
With laughter ringing through the clear air,
Nature's comedy show was beyond compare.

As twilight fell, the fun didn't cease,
With a woodland dance, each heart found peace.
In the whispers of leaves, joy took wing,
Celebrating the magic that laughter can bring.

Horizons Beyond the Bark

A beaver in shades, with a clever plan,
Tried to build a boat, but it sank like a pan.
His buddies all laughed from the grassy shore,
Saying, "Stick to dams, you're good at galore!"

A flamboyant fox strutted with pride,
Flipping his tail, looking dignified.
He slipped on a banana peel, oh what a mess,
Tumbling down, leaving all in distress.

The butterflies giggled, flapping their wings,
As they witnessed the chaos that friendship brings.
The trees swayed gently, in laughter they shook,
As the sun set slowly, casting a hook.

With the stars peeking down from the sky so dark,
They all shared tales of joy, a true lark.
In this woodland theatre, beneath the moonlight,
Laughter echoed, a pure delight.

Verdant Whispers Above

In the boughs high up, a party was brewing,
With animals dressed in costumes, all glowing.
A gopher in stripes was DJ for the night,
Mixing dance moves to the moon's silver light.

A goat on the drums kept the beat alive,
While fireflies flashed, making all thrive.
A squirrel stood up, to give a toast,
"To our woodland friends! Let's cheer and boast!"

With each little bump and tumble from fun,
The gopher yelled out, "Come and join, everyone!"
The trees all swayed to their wild music,
As laughter spilled out, a real acoustic.

As dawn approached, they danced even more,
In the cool morning breeze, spirits to soar.
In the ballet of nature, all spirits were free,
In the laughter of woods, joy was the key.

Tales from the Verdant Abyss

A squirrel with a silly hat,
Danced on a branch, what of that?
He tripped and fell into a nest,
Where birds thought him their honored guest.

A chipmunk juggled nuts in a line,
While mocking the owl, 'I am divine!'
But the owl just rolled his wise old eyes,
And muttered, 'This critter tells big lies.'

A frog in a tie croaked out a tune,
With the sun shining bright like a cartoon.
He sang to the trees, the bees chimed in,
While munching on flies, with a cheeky grin.

A raccoon played poker, bluffing his hand,
Against a young rabbit who couldn't stand.
When cards flew and snacks were all around,
It ended in laughter, no winner found.

Legends of the Lingering Breeze

The breeze tickled leaves in a playful way,
As a parrot squawked, 'I'm king of the day!'
He preened all his feathers with flair and pride,
While nearby, a lizard just laughed and sighed.

A hedgehog, quite dapper in shoes made of grass,
Tried to impress a young turtle, alas!
He tripped on a twig and twirled on his back,
And everyone giggled at his funny act.

The clouds floated by, like fluffy old sheep,
While raccoons held karaoke, not missing a beat.
Their voices were sharp, a cacophony made,
Yet all who heard danced in a joyous parade.

The ants threw a bash with crumbs they could find,
As fireflies lit up the scene, oh so kind!
They jived in a circle around a small tree,
And life in the woods turned wild and free.

Whispers of the Canopy

A gentle breeze told tales of the wild,
Of rabbits in suits and a cat that smiled.
An acorn wore glasses, pretended to read,
While squirrels debated who'd win the speed.

A sloth in a hammock, napping with flair,
Dreamed of adventures he'd love if aware.
But when he awoke, stretched and said, 'Meh!'
He just grabbed a snack and then nodded 'Okay.'

The frogs held a race to splash and to croak,
With mud on their faces, they jumped and they joked.
The winner, a grumpy old toad named Lou,
Just shrugged and said, 'What's a trophy to do?'

The owls played chess with the night as their cloak,
While bats hung around, sharing jokes that provoke.
With giggles and hoots filling up the night air,
The forest has secrets, but it's hard not to share.

Echoes from the Branches

In the heart of the woods, where the wild things laugh,
A bear on a skateboard found his weird path.
He wobbled and gurgled with each little push,
Till he crashed and rolled in a soft mountain bush.

A spider spun webs that sparkled and danced,
While nearby a rabbit dreamed deep in a trance.
The webs caught the dew, twinkling like stars,
And the rabbit awoke, ready for bizarre.

A chorus of critters, both furry and bright,
Held a talent show under the moonlight.
With juggling and singing and acts that astound,
The evening grew wild with joy all around.

A raccoon with a trumpet played tunes from his heart,
The sound echoed joyfully, a comedy art.
The night carried laughter, like seeds on the breeze,
In the branches, they whispered, 'Oh, can't you see?'

The Skyward Sanctuary

Squirrels bounce like tiny clowns,
Chasing leaves in silly crowns.
A raccoon sings a catchy tune,
While birds dance under a bright balloon.

The branches sway, a leafy stage,
Where chipmunks laugh and squirrels rage.
Each gust of wind brings a surprise,
As acorns fall like little pies.

Frogs in hats perform a show,
While bees put on their own cabaret glow.
The sun peeks through with a cheeky grin,
Inviting all to join the spin.

Nature's playground, high and wild,
A treehouse realm for every child.
With giggles echoing through the grove,
In this merry place, we laugh and rove.

Echoes from the Arboreal Realm

In lofty heights, the laughter trails,
Where jays wear hats and tell the tales.
A wise old owl gives a wink,
As squirrels nod, and giggles sync.

A rabbit jumps from branch to branch,
With floppy ears, he starts to prance.
The winds whistle a jig so sweet,
While raccoons tap their dancing feet.

The leaves whisper jokes to the breeze,
As owls hoot out their own puns with ease.
Each rustling sound brings a hearty cheer,
In this woodsy realm, joy is near.

From boughs above, a chorus sings,
Of mischievous dreams and silly flings.
With every heartbeat, the forest plays,
In echoes of laughter, it sways and sways.

Adventures in the Branches

A squirrel dons a pirate hat,
And challenges a crow for a slice of cheese spat.
The acorn cannon, they devise,
Fly through the air like wondrous pies!

Down below, the rabbits chase,
A butterfly, all over the place.
They tumble and roll in patches of grass,
While bees shout cheers as they pass.

A frog in shades relaxes by,
As all the critters laugh and sigh.
With every leap, a joke takes wing,
In this tree-top land, where the laughers sing.

The sun dips low, with a wink and a nod,
As we dance through shadows, a joyful squad.
Up in the trees, we find delight,
In silly adventures from morning 'til night.

Legends Beneath the Canopy

The tales of chipmunks fill the air,
With acorn quests and nutty flair.
A daring heist by ghostly bats,
Results in giggles from the chitchat chats.

An old tree trunk tells its lore,
Of silly mishaps from yesteryear's score.
Kingfisher winks, and all eyes meet,
As frogs leap forth with a playful beat.

Beneath the canopy, laughter reigns,
With wacky dances in colorful chains.
Every rustle spins a brand new myth,
In this verdant realm, joy is a gift.

And when the stars sprinkle the night,
The tales continue, a pure delight.
In nature's embrace, where fun abounds,
The legends of laughter are forever found.

Dreams in the Foliage

Squirrels debate who can climb high,
While owls on branches all watch and sigh.
A raccoon in a hat made of leaves,
Claims he knows secrets that nobody believes.

The wind whispers jokes as it tickles the bark,
While chipmunks gather, their laughter a spark.
A parrot recites lines from a play,
As the sun sets to end another wild day.

Beneath the canopy, a dance starts to bloom,
With fireflies twinkling, dispelling the gloom.
Frogs in top hats hop, oh what a sight!
Nature's own comedy, oh what a delight!

Underneath stars, the fun never stops,
Stories exchange as the laughter just pops.
In dreams of the foliage, joy takes its flight,
Every creature can join in the whimsical night.

Journey to the Crown

A rabbit with goggles sets off to the skies,
Flapping his ears while he giggles and flies.
He meets a wise owl who hoots with a grin,
"Journey to the crown? Let the fun begin!"

Swinging from branches, a monkey appears,
Telling tall tales, full of laughter and cheers.
Raccoons wearing ties scurry by with a wink,
While squirrels play trumpets, oh how they think!

Through blossoms and vines, the path twists and turns,
With each nutty misstep, the heart brightly burns.
An unforeseen slide sends them all in a spin,
Laughter erupts as they tumble, oh win!

At the crown of the tree, they finally rest,
Chowing down snacks, oh they're truly blessed.
Dreams and wild stories beam from their eyes,
In this journey of laughter, they reach for the skies.

The Vibrance of Higher Realms

Breezes carry giggles through branches so tall,
While bees in their hives start to sing and to brawl.
A butterfly dressed in a polka-dot gown,
Waltzes with flowers in her bright flowery town.

The sunbeams slip in for a playful surprise,
As acorns compete in their nutty disguise.
A woodpecker drums in a dance on the square,
Creating a rhythm that draws giggles and flair.

Up high in the canopy, colors collide,
Each critter contributes, not one tries to hide.
Laughter erupts with each twist and each turn,
In this lively realm where your heart can just churn.

As twilight descends, the stars start to peek,
Creatures now sit for a chat, oh so cheek.
Their whispers float softly on the night's gentle breeze,
In high, vibrant realms, they find joy and ease.

Nature's Voices Above

In the chatter of leaves, a cantankerous choir,
Each rustle and crackle, a symphony of fire.
The cheeky raccoons throw a musical fit,
While birds take the stage and refuse to sit.

A lazy sloth strums on a branch with such grace,
While squirrels provide harmony, quickening the pace.
A turtle in shades offers riffs that astound,
With laughter erupting at every sweet sound.

The sun gently dims in a soft, rosy glow,
As night creatures rise to steal the show.
Crickets provide beats, while owls hoot in tune,
Their voices weave stories beneath the bright moon.

In this orchestra grand, you can't help but grin,
Where joy and confusion blend thick as a pin.
Nature's own laughter, a sweet symphony found,
Echoes above, where adventure abounds.

Whispers Among the Leaves

In the branches, critters peek,
Squirrels chatter, quite the cheek.
A frog hops up, wearing a hat,
He croaks a tune, and sits down flat.

A parrot squawks with wicked glee,
"Who's that down there? Come dance with me!"
The raccoon joins, a dance so spry,
While ants march by, they shout, "Oh my!"

The winds carry giggles, a joyous sound,
As acorns tumble softly down.
Each leaf tells jokes, a leafy sprawl,
Laughter echoes, embracing all.

So under the canopy, life is grand,
With silly friends, a merry band.
In every rustle, a story sways,
In this green world, it's always play.

Canopy Chronicles

On branches high, a sloth takes a nap,
But little birds plot a clever trap.
They drop pranks, like seeds in spring,
And wake him up to see what's bling!

A squirrel spins tales of treasure near,
While chipmunks cheer, their eyes full of cheer.
"Did you see the glimpse of that shiny thing?"
They whisper of stories, adventure's zing!

A raccoon tells tales of a daring heist,
Stealing berries from the picnic, oh so nice!
His eyes gleam bright with mischief bold,
As the forest holds its breath, secrets untold.

In this tree realm, gossip takes flight,
Making every day a pure delight.
Nature's jesters, in a leafy fest,
In this high playground, they are the best!

Secrets of the Upper Boughs

In the upper limbs, a hoot and a howl,
An owl sings out to the playful prowl.
A monkey swings by, with curious grace,
Chasing shadows, at a merry pace.

"Who stole my nuts?" cried the squirrel in glee,
A raccoon sneers, "Not me, come see!"
With a flick of the tail, fun stories arise,
In every nook, a surprise that lies!

A chattering group of ladybugs chat,
While a wise old tortoise wears his hat.
"What's the buzz, my friends? Was it you?"
In the tree tops, mysteries ensue!

When twilight wraps the branches tight,
The stars flicker, twinkling bright.
In the night, they spin their yarns,
Of laughter, pranks, and silly charms.

Flight of the Feathered Stories

Birds gather round for a tale or two,
A pigeon starts with, "So, here's what I knew!"
A seagull chimes in with a squawk and a spin,
As the woodpecker taps, "Let's begin!"

"Once there was a fox who dreamed of flight,
He fashioned some wings in the pale moonlight!
He jumped from a rock, oh what a sight,
But just went boom! Not quite right!"

Chirps of laughter echoed so wide,
Each feathered friend bursting with pride.
The tales of folly, they surely delight,
In this high world, everything's bright.

With a flutter, they dance in the breeze,
Crafting funny tales with such ease.
In the trees, they share their fun,
Under a sky where dreams just run.

Adventures in the Luminescent Grove

In a grove where glowbugs dance,
Trees wear hats, not left to chance.
Squirrels jump like acrobats,
Chasing shadows, pouncing cats.

A raccoon holds a tea-time chat,
With owls dressed in a fancy hat.
Frogs play cards, decked out with glee,
While fireflies hum a melody.

Mice sip juice from acorn cups,
Expecting wise old tree to sup.
Branches play a game of hide,
As chipmunks take their silly ride.

Giggles echo through the air,
With every twist of nature's flair.
In this grove, the fun won't end,
Every twist is a funny bend.

The Timberline Outpour

At the top where the tall trees sway,
Critters plot their silly play.
A beaver dances on a log,
While a fox prances, dressed like a dog.

Woodpeckers drum a funky beat,
Mice tap dance with flapping feet.
The wind carries laughter so bright,
Even bats join in, taking flight.

Trees gossip, whispering low,
About raccoons stealing the show.
The laughter branches far and wide,
In the timber where jokes reside.

A bear slips on berries, oh what grace,
Falling flat on his fuzzy face!
Yet mirth rings out, a playful sound,
In this high place where joy is found.

Hushed Stories of Perched Beings

In a bough where stories thrive,
Birds tweet tales that come alive.
A parrot recounts an old balloon,
While sparrows snicker under the moon.

An owl winks, gives a sly grin,
Says he knows where the best jokes have been.
A canary sings of a cat's big fall,
As laughter bounces, echoing all.

Chicks chirp tales of thunderous glee,
About a tree that danced like a spree.
Every branch holds secrets in cheer,
While the night sky listens near.

With each verse, the fun unfolds,
In a hush, every story told.
Perched beings weave a merry tune,
Under the watchful, smiling moon.

The Boughs' Quiet Murmurs

In the boughs where whispers play,
Trees laugh softly through the day.
A chipmunk juggles shiny bits,
While a crow squawks and tries to sit.

Breezes carry silly jests,
As petals dress in leaf-shaped vests.
Squirrels debate on nutty snacks,
Plotting pranks, avoiding cracks.

With twigs as swords, they duel in jest,
Nature's heroes, never at rest.
Boughs chuckle at the games they see,
Making mischief, oh so free.

Each chatter adds to the fun's delight,
Even shadows join in the night.
In the quiet hum of woodlands' calls,
The laughter dances, and joy befalls.

A Sojourn in the Canopy

Squirrels in suits with ties so neat,
They hold meetings and take their seat.
Chattering loudly, they pitch a grand plan,
To steal some acorns, their army, a clan.

A wise old owl, perched high up above,
Winks at the chaos, oh, how he loves!
'Who's running this show?' he hoots with a grin,
As nutty debates commence from within.

A parade of ants in a line so fine,
Marching for berries, their target divine.
They trip and they tumble; it's quite the sight,
Those little mischief-makers, full of delight.

And when the sun sets, the stars are aglow,
The creatures retreat, ready to stow.
Yet whispers of giggles float through the leaves,
As dreams of the canopy spin and weave.

Parables of the Lofty Grove

A raccoon once wore a hat and a shoe,
Thinking it clever, full of virtue.
Neighbors all chuckled, 'He's lost his way!'
But he danced in the moonlight, hip-hip-hooray!

There's a parrot who raps on a tree branch bold,
Spitting sweet rhymes, full of gold.
He boasts of great feats through the evening air,
But forgets his own verses, getting lost in despair.

A turtle on stilts tries to waltz with finesse,
Stumbles and grumbles, oh what a mess!
With laughter around him, he shrugs it off,
The rhythm is shaky, but he gives a scoff.

Finally, the stars gather close at night,
Whispering secrets, sharing delight.
In the grove, tales twist, laughter rings free,
With each story told, it's pure jubilee!

From Branch to Heart

A chameleon sitting, stuck in a tree,
Changes his colors for all to see.
When someone asks, 'What shade is that?'
He mumbles and fumbles, gets caught in a spat.

A pair of owls, one fuzzy, one wise,
Try to impress all the stars in the skies.
One hoots in jest, 'I know all the facts!'
The other just snickers, 'You're lost in your acts!'

Green-cheeked parrots spin tales on a swing,
Their gossip as loud as they flap and they sing.
They chatter and cackle, it's all just for fun,
Each story a flight, under rays of the sun.

As night gently falls, the ruckus will cease,
The creatures all gather, their laughter's a feast.
From branch to heart, they spread joy all around,
In the woodland high up, where giggles abound.

The Arboreal Diaries

In bark-bound volumes, secrets do dwell,
Written by creatures with stories to tell.
A chipmunk named Charlie pens tales of delight,
Of berry mishaps that last through the night.

There's a mischievous bat with a whimsical plot,
Who dreams of adventures, a daring little tot.
He swoops and he dives with comedic finesse,
Until he mistakenly lands in a dress!

Frogs hold court, with croaks and with laughs,
Sharing their best jokes like skilled little gaffes.
Each ribbit a punchline, under the moon's glow,
Jokes of the pond, a humorous show.

When all's said and done, as stories unwind,
The creatures together, in laughter they bind.
Pages turn nightly, as joy fills the trees,
In diaries scattered, where giggles tease.

The High Perch Narratives

A squirrel swings in a hat too big,
He claims he's a knight, does a silly jig.
The birds all laugh from their branches high,
As the knight nearly takes to the sky.

With acorns for armor and sticks for swords,
He challenges cats, his baffling lords.
A tumble ensues, the ribbing begins,
As he lands on a nest, where a chickadee grins.

He squeaks with glee, 'What a bold duel!'
But the cats just purr, and that's how they rule.
The knight shakes it off, with a dramatic flair,
Then bows to the crowd, unaware of the air.

So remember this tale of valor and pride,
Upon leafy thrones, with squirrels as guides.
For in high places where giggles curl,
A knight in a hat can inspire a whirl.

Ballads of the Boughs

In branches thick, a tale unfolds,
Of a parrot who claims he's the one who holds.
With feathers bright and a beak so loud,
He hosts poetry nights, drawing in a crowd.

A raccoon shows up with snacks galore,
While a wise old owl reads poetry lore.
They snicker and squabble, all in good cheer,
As the parrot declares, 'Let's all drink some beer!'

But instead it's berry juice, a fruity delight,
With hiccups and laughter, they party all night.
A misfit band on a leafy stage,
Their whimsical antics, a true circus page.

So sing loud in trees where the wild critters play,
For every great ballad hides humor at bay.
In the heart of the boughs, where silliness grows,
The laughter of nature is everybody's prose.

Treasures at Twilit Heights

At twilight's gleam, where shadows creep,
A chipmunk stashes treasures to keep.
But in his dreams of gold and fame,
He finds only acorns, never the same.

With a glittery leaf, he hears a loud hum,
The big bees arrive, with a graceful thrum.
They've smelled the snacks, his bounty so sweet,
And soon they're buzzing, making a feast!

He yells, 'Hey, wait! This isn't for you!'
But they dance 'round his head, like a merry crew.
In a twist of fate, he now joins their song,
A joyous jam where all critters belong.

So under the stars, 'round the twiggy glow,
The best of surprises are treasures we know.
At heights so twilit, where daylight flees,
Magic abounds in the rustling leaves.

Harmony of the Higher Heights

In the upper branches, where the sun likes to play,
A chorus arises from critters at sway.
A frog sings bass, while the sparrows squawk,
Creating a symphony on their tree-top walk.

'No off-key notes!' the wise owl gives shout,
As the raccoon joins in with a wink and a pout.
'Keep it together!' the squirrel jumps high,
While giggles erupt from the clouds in the sky.

The songbirds flit with their melodious cheer,
While leaves rustle softly, their rhythm so clear.
A harmony builds with each chirp and croak,
As nighttime approaches, the laughter won't choke.

So dance in the treetops, partake in the fun,
For the music of life has only begun.
In heights where we frolic, our spirits take flight,
With the world beneath us glowing golden and bright.

Chronicle of the Emerald Heights

In the emerald crowns, squirrels debate,
Whose acorn is best? And who's just late?
The wise old owl snores, misses the show,
While ants in a conga line steal the glow.

The chipmunks perform a grand circus act,
Spinning on branches, a sight to unpack!
But one little critter falls flat on his face,
Turns red as a cherry, oh what a disgrace!

Nuts fly like missiles in a feathery fray,
As birds sing in harmony, "Let's join the play!"
A swing on a branch becomes quite the ride,
With laughter that echoes through tree trunks so wide.

When sunlight descends, the antics will cease,
As night wraps the forest in a velvet fleece.
But wait for tomorrow, more mischief in store,
In the emerald heights, there's always much more!

Whistling Woods and Soft Hues

In Whistling Woods, the trees start to hum,
As raccoons recite poems, just for fun.
With hats made of leaves, they dance 'round and shake,
While the bushes all giggle, making the ground quake.

A fox joins the frolic, with shoes made of vines,
He twirls and he whirls, crossing all the lines.
His tail trips the squirrel, who tumbles with flair,
"Just practice!" he chuckles, with a mischievous stare.

The flowers all blushed in their pastel attire,
As the sun shines down, igniting their fire.
A breeze carries notes of the laughter and clinks,
When the porcupines toast with their prickly drinks.

Oh, what a gathering! Under skies painted blue,
The woods come alive with every wacky view.
So join the parade, where fun never ends,
In Whistling Woods, where mischief transcends!

Fables on the Fronds

On fronds above, where laughter takes flight,
Frogs tell tall tales, oh what a sight!
A turtle in glasses, with wisdom profound,
Sips tea with the robins, all gathered around.

The lizards hold contests on who's the best sprinter,
While the butterflies flitter, like rays from a printer.
Each leap and each flutter, a wacky display,
As nature's own stage, unfolds day by day.

Bees join in singing, a tune quite absurd,
As dragonflies dart, their laughter is heard.
But watch out for Ladybug, queen of the scene,
Who's marking her territory, bold and serene.

With shadows growing long, the antics must end,
But tomorrow awaits, fun and mischief will blend.
On fronds of imagination, where joy meets the breeze,
The fables continue, oh what a tease!

Sagas in the Sky

Above in the branches, the band starts to play,
With raccoons on drums, what a wild display!
A parrot does solos, so funky and bright,
While the crows in tuxedos cheer through the night.

The party's in full swing, the moon shining wide,
As a hedgehog named Spike takes a dizzying ride.
Spinning and twirling, he lost all his pride,
Rolling down branches and crashing with pride.

The stars wink and giggle, giving their cheer,
As bumpkin-spirits rise, spilling joy far and near.
Each tale told is wilder than the one from before,
Where laughter is currency, and fun is the score.

But as dawn approaches, the party winds down,
With yawns, and soft sighs, from critters around.
Under skies of adventure, where giggles don't die,
The sagas keep growing, in the branches up high.

Secrets of the Sunlit Canopy

In the branches, squirrels dance,
Pinecones rain down by chance.
A bird sings low, a joke unfurled,
While a chipmunk grins, the king of the world.

Leaves rustle with gossip, oh such fun,
"Did you see the rabbit? He thinks he's the one!"
The sun peeks in, a playful spy,
While shadows giggle and time drifts by.

A caterpillar whispers a silly rhyme,
"Why don't trees ever play cards? Too much time!"
The branches chuckle, the wind gives a shove,
"Everyone knows, they're sure to get above!"

In this high tale, laughter's the air,
Bouncing along without a care.
Each fluttering leaf, a quirk or jest,
In the canopy's heart, there's never a rest.

The Perch of Possibilities

High above, the world looks small,
A crow's loud laugh rings through it all.
"From up here, I could be a star!
Or just a bird with a nutty memoir!"

The branches sway, a trampoline's thrill,
"Watch me flip! I can't keep still!"
While ants march on, they tiptoe and strut,
"Watch your step! Or you'll end up in a nut!"

A wise old owl, eyes like moons,
Tells squirrel stories and silly tunes.
"Why did the tree break up with its mate?
Too many limbs, it couldn't relate!"

In this lofty space, humor finds a seat,
Every giggle, a branch downbeat.
The world below is like a big joke,
As the sun sets, the laughter awoke.

Flights of Fancy Among the Leaves

Up here among the rustling green,
Every critter has a quirky scene.
A squirrel complains of a nutty plight,
"Why do they roll? I can't hold it tight!"

The woodpecker taps with rhythm divine,
"Join my band, let's make some sunshine!"
A fluttering butterfly flits by with flair,
"Catch me if you can; it's all in the air!"

A whispering breeze carries tales of fun,
"Did you hear? The fox was trying to run!"
The leaves emit giggles, a musical score,
While shadows sway, asking for more.

Every twist and turn, a delightful new jest,
In a bright world, where laughter's the best.
As stars peek in, the fun ignites,
In the heart of the leaves, joy takes flight.

Voices from the Vantage Point

Perched high, where the world can't reach,
The branches gather to play and teach.
A little bird chirps, "I'm a froggy knight!
In search of a lunch that's out of sight!"

"Why so serious?" asks the bright green vine,
"Breathe in the fun, let laughter align."
The day's full of jokes, a comic spree,
Even the leaves join in, full of glee.

A beaver floats by, on a log so wide,
"Why don't trees ever swim? They slide to the side!"
The chorus of chuckles echoes so free,
"Let's start a band, who's got the key?"

In this view, where mischief abounds,
Joy is the treasure that always surrounds.
Each silly moment, a gem on display,
In the carefree heights, we dance and sway.

Chronicles Written in Green

In the branches, squirrels chat,
Trading secrets while they gnaw on fat.
A parrot mimics, oh what a joust,
Every sound, a flutter of a boast.

A raccoon snickers, swipes some nuts,
Claiming dinner from the feathered ruts.
The woodpecker drums a silly beat,
Each peck a giggle, oh so sweet.

Frogs leap high and land with a thunk,
While the shadows dance to banjos sunk.
A lizard lounges, sipping on dew,
Says, "Life's a breeze—come join the crew!"

In green jungles, laughter bangs,
As nature hums her joyful clangs.
It's a circus up above, come see,
The comedy club of the tallest tree!

The Pulse of the Canopy

Up in the branches, the chorus calls,
A band of critters on leafy halls.
The owls hoot with their wise old eyes,
As the raccoons plot their midnight highs.

Squirrels pirouette, tails held so high,
Chasing each other in zig-zaggy spry.
While the monkeys swing with cheeky glee,
Whispering jokes that only they see.

Ants march on, a diligent crew,
Carrying crumbs like they're kings anew.
But oops! One trips, a tumble so grand,
It makes the whole trail stop and stand.

Underneath the swaying green stage,
The laughter echoes, it's the new age.
From branches high to roots that sway,
It's a funny world in leafy play!

Flickers of Life Above Ground

A butterfly dances, flits with flair,
While a grasshopper's concert fills the air.
Fireflies twinkle, all aglow,
A festival of lights with nature's show.

The sun peeks in, a playful tease,
Casting shadows as it sways with ease.
A crow cracks jokes from a splintered limb,
Dodging acorns that seem to brim.

Chirping crickets with jokes untold,
They share their secrets, brave and bold.
A carnival of life, up we go,
In this green world, laughter steals the show.

So join the fun, take a peek and see,
The vibrant life among the trees.
With giggles and grins, we'll take a chance,
In the grandest, quirkiest tree-top dance!

Roosting with Nature's Lore

A wise old owl, with feathers so bright,
Shares tales of the day, woven with delight.
The sun sets low, casting deep hues,
While squirrels play games in the twilight blues.

A buzzing bee shares buzzing news,
Of flowers blooming in the dew.
While raccoons giggle, plotting their heist,
As they eye the picnic, oh what a feast!

The laughter grows, as shadows merge,
With each bark and chirp, the stories surge.
The wind whips through, joining the glee,
With merry beats from the tallest tree.

Roosting here, under the starry sky,
Nature's lore makes the night fly by.
With a wink and a nudge, the critters adore,
The funny tales of life, forevermore!

Sagas from the Canopied Heights

In leafy realms where squirrels scheme,
A raccoon wakes from a mischieve dream.
He tries to steal a birdseed sack,
But ends up stuck—oh, what a hack!

Upon a branch, a parrot squawks,
While trying on his neighbor's socks.
The owls roll their eyes in delight,
As antics unfold in morning light.

A woodpecker starts a raucous tune,
Banging his drum beneath the moon.
The trees all dance with branches wavy,
While creatures cheer—oh, how they're crazy!

In the canopy, laughter's the goal,
Where giggles rise and young hearts bowl.
Each tale told, with a wink and a cheer,
In this green world, we hold dear!

When Trees Speak

Whispers soft from giants above,
Sharing secrets just like a dove.
A pine grumbles, "Get off my shade!"
While willows giggle—a grand charade!

The birch with bark that peels and flakes,
Teases the oak, "You're full of aches!"
"Oh please," laughs the sturdy old friend,
"I've stood high here—I won't bend!"

Maples argue over syrup's flow,
"Mine is sweetest!" one shouts in the show.
While squirrels stifle a breathless cheer,
What a conversation—a tree frontier!

As the leaves shake in playful jeers,
They settle down; we lend them our ears.
In laughter or tales, let them speak,
For wisdom flows where branches peek!

Celestial Canopy

Up high in skies so wild and free,
Stars twinkle down among the trees.
A chameleon plays hide-and-seek,
While frogs sing tunes that make you peak!

Mice hold rallies in moonlit glades,
Debating who can toss the best blades.
The fireflies join with a flashing light,
Creating a disco—oh, what a sight!

A hedgehog dances with a funky paw,
Claiming that he's the best by law.
Yet everyone knows that it's quite the blend,
In this wild party that'll never end!

Branches sway as the winds play along,
With branches drumming a heartwarming song.
The canopy gleams with laughter and cheer,
In this dreamy oasis, we hold dear!

Tales in the Shade

In cozy nooks where shadows lie,
A few old leaves glance up to the sky.
"Tell a story!" whispers the breeze,
While a lazy chipmunk munches with ease.

A young sapling dreams of heights to climb,
While ants march in a perfect line.
They talk of berries, good times ahead,
In laughter and joy, they're truly fed!

A grasshopper leaps with a mighty hop,
Lamenting dreams that just can't stop.
"Oh, to be grand!" he sings in delight,
But all his pals say, "You're just right!"

As stories spin in the dappled shade,
With chuckles and giggles that never fade.
In this woodland space, we find our place,
With heart and laughter, a warm embrace!

The High-Altitude Chronicles

Up in the branches where squirrels do sway,
Chasing their tails in a playful ballet.
One nut, two nuts, then off they go,
Swinging like acrobats, just putting on a show.

A bird with a hat says, "What a fine day!"
While a chipmunk below thinks he's king of the hay.
He struts and he poses, all swollen with pride,
Until he trips over and tumbles aside.

The breeze whispers secrets to leaves in a rush,
While a frog on a branch gives a grumpy old hush.
"Keep it down, you walkers, on roots with your feet,
For I'm trying to nap, not skydive from my seat!"

When night falls, the owls gather round,
Trading wisecracks and jokes as they sound.
Their laughter echoes high, through branches it weaves,
In this forest of folly, where nonsense believes.

Fluttering Pages of Nature

A butterfly flaps with a rumor so loud,
She thinks she's the queen, drawing in a crowd.
"Look at my colors, my wings, feel the breeze!"
But a twig snaps beneath her – oh, squeal like a tease!

Next, a raccoon with a curious glance,
Tries to put on a pair of old tree pants.
"I'm the trendsetter, wait 'til you see!
With pockets for snacks, it's all about me!"

A clever little fox plays tricks with a wink,
Setting up pranks quicker than you could think.
"Why did the owl sit on the branch?" he'll say,
"Because the light bulb wasn't burning today!"

As daylight fades into a chuckle and cheer,
The forest unfolds, and the laughter draws near.
For every leaf rustles, there's a story to know,
In this wild, funny world, where all the critters glow.

Tints of Dawn and Dusk

At dawn, the woodpecker taps with such flair,
Saying "Wake up, sleepyheads, come out for fresh air!"
He hammers a rhythm, then stops with a pause,
To strike a pose, pretending he's Claus.

As day turns to dusk, the sun starts to yawn,
A raccoon flips pancakes on the dew-laden lawn.
"Who said nuts and berries can't be served warm?
Just wait 'til you taste my maple syrup swarm!"

Fireflies emerge, with their twinkling lights,
They dance like little candles on summer nights.
A moth tries to join, but gets tangled in threads,
Chasing those flickers, he tumbles on heads!

With the moon up high and the giggles so sweet,
Every creature will laugh in this cozy retreat.
Nature's a storyteller, funny and bright,
As dusk giggles on, with delight in its flight.

Where Foliage Meets the Sky

The branches reach high, like arms in a race,
While the raccoons debate if they're first or last place.
"Let's climb to the top!" one shouts with great glee,
But the branches just wobble, "Not that way, we plea!"

A parrot in glasses reads stories aloud,
To the critters below, each one in a crowd.
"Once there was a cat who fancied a tree,
But he climbed up too fast, and now, can't you see?"

The hedgehog is thinking, "How do I fit in?
With the squirrels so spry, I feel like a pin!"
But then he rolls over, and with such a great cheer,
Bounces into a pile, the laughter draws near!

From sunup to sundown, in branches so spry,
There's magic and mischief where foliage meets sky.
Each day tells a story, each night a new grin,
In this treetop comedy, the fun never thins.

www.ingramcontent.com/pod-product-compliance
Lightning Source LLC
Chambersburg PA
CBHW071814160426
43209CB00003B/81